ENGLISH LANGUAGE ARTS
HOMESCHOOL CURRICULUM WORKBOOK
GRADE 9

by Laura Daly

Contact the author:
writeandreadteacher.com
@writeandreadteacher

TABLE OF CONTENTS

Instructions for Use...5

Fiction Unit

Elements of Fiction Reference Guide...6-8

"The Cask of Amontillado" Short Story...9-18

"The Cask of Amontillado" Irony Chart...19

"The Cask of Amontillado" Writing Prompt...20

"The Cask of Amontillado" Test Your Knowledge...21-22

"The Gift of the Magi" Short Story...23-29

"The Gift of the Magi" Theme Chart...30

"The Gift of the Magi" SIFT Chart..31

"The Gift of the Magi" Writing Prompt..32

"The Gift of the Magi" Test Your Knowledge..33-34

Grammar Unit

Semicolon Reference Guide..35

Colon Reference Guide...36

Using Semicolons...37

Using Colons..38

Semicolons and Colons..39

Semicolon and Colons: Test Your Knowledge...40

Rhetorical Analysis Unit

Rhetoric Reference Guide...41

Rhetorical Appeals in Advertising..42

Selling with Rhetorical Appeals...43-44

Rhetorical Appeals: Test Your Knowledge...45

Speech Background Information..46

Statement on the Assassination of Martin Luther King Jr................................47-48

SOAPSTone Chart..49

Rhetorical Appeals Chart..50

Literary Devices Chart...51

Writing a Rhetorical Analysis..52

Rhetorical Analysis Graphic Organizers...53-57

Nonfiction Text Structures and Features Unit

Nonfiction Text Structures Reference Guide..58

TABLE OF CONTENTS

Nonfiction Text Features Reference Guide..59

"Stealing Lincoln's Body" Nonfiction Text..60-61

"Stealing Lincoln's Body" Questions and Timeline..62-63

"Cell Phones in the Classroom: Beneficial or Detrimental?" Nonfiction Text..........64-65

"Cell Phones in the Classroom: Beneficial or Detrimental?" Questions.............66

"Cell Phones in the Classroom: Beneficial or Detrimental?" Pros and Cons.........67

Argumentative Writing Unit

Argumentative Writing Reference Guide...68

Sample Argument Essay..69-70

Examining an Argument Essay..71

Choosing an Argumentative Essay Topic...72

Argument Essay Graphic Organizers..73-77

Poetry Unit

Poetry Terms Reference Guide..78-82

"I Never Saw a Moor" Poem and Questions...83-85

"I Never Saw a Moor" Writing Prompt..86

"Stopping by Woods on a Snowy Evening" Poem and Questions....................87-89

"Stopping by Woods on a Snowy Evening" Writing Prompt.............................90

Novel Unit

Independent Reading Introduction..91

Novel Playlist Book Project...92-95

Answer Keys

Answer Keys and Sample Answers...96-103

INSTRUCTIONS FOR USE

This English 9 curriculum workbook is designed for single use so students can work directly inside the workbook. Lessons are aligned with Common Core standards for grade 9 and serve as a curriculum option for homeschooling families. It is a rigorous and engaging alternative to traditional schooling.

There are seven units within the workbook. At the beginning of each unit, students will find reference sheets with important vocabulary and examples. If your child ever struggles with questions or writing prompts, have them revisit the reference pages for the key vocabulary.

Lessons are to be completed in order as some content builds to support later assignments. Completing the work sequentially will eliminate confusion and missed skills.

Although this curriculum is designed to replace a year of traditional English 9, I strongly suggest that your child reads books of their choosing throughout the year as well. This curriculum includes one independent reading project, but reading regularly is recommended. You can visit your local public library for a wide book selection.

Answer keys are located in the back of the workbook. It does include sample answers for open ended questions. If you want control over the answer keys while your child is working, feel free to tear those pages out of the workbook.

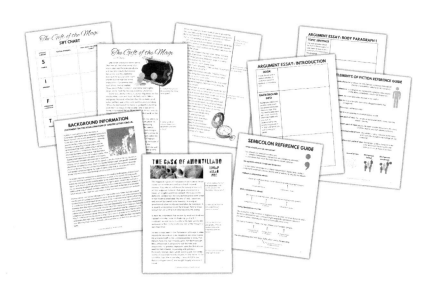

ELEMENTS OF FICTION REFERENCE GUIDE

conflict: a struggle or problem in a story

plot: the sequence of events that make up a story

   exposition: the beginning of a story that includes background information to help the reader understand the story

   rising action: the series of events that lead to the climax

   climax: the point at which the action reaches its peak

   falling action: the series of events that lead to the resolution

   resolution: the end of the story when the main conflict is resolved

PLOT DIAGRAM

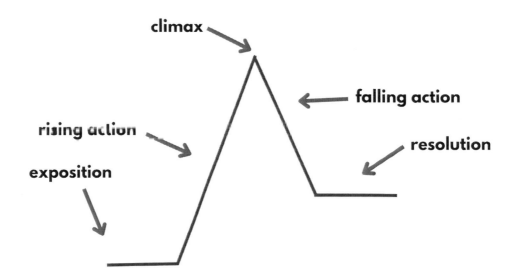

setting: when and where the story occurs

characterization: the methods a writer uses to develop characters

ELEMENTS OF FICTION REFERENCE GUIDE

dynamic character: a character who changes and grows throughout the story (sometimes called a round character)

static character: a character that remains the same over the course of the story (sometimes called a flat character)

protagonist: the main character involved in the conflict

antagonist: the character who opposes or struggles against the protagonist

narrator: the person telling the story

point of view: the perspective from which a story is told

   first person point of view: the narrator is a character in the story, uses the words I, me, my

   second person point of view: you as the reader are the character in the story, used for choose your own adventure books

   third person limited point of view: the narrator is not a character in the story and knows the thoughts and feelings of one character

   third person omniscient point of view: the narrator is not a character in the story and knows the thoughts and feelings of two or more characters

first person

second person

third person limited

third person omniscient

ELEMENTS OF FICTION REFERENCE GUIDE

tone: a writer or speaker's attitude towards a subject

mood: the atmosphere or general feeling of the story

theme: a writer's central idea or main message about life (themes are not directly stated in the text)

dramatic irony: form of irony in which the reader knows more about future events than the characters

verbal irony: form of irony that occurs when a character or narrator says one thing but means something else

situational irony: form of irony that occurs when a character or reader expects one thing to happen, but something else happens instead

motif: a recurring image, symbol, theme, character type, or subject within a story

symbol: something that has its own meaning but also stands for something else on a figurative level

This is an olive branch. It is often used as a symbol of peace.

foreshadowing: hints or clues that suggest future action in a story

allusion: a reference to a well-known person, place, or event from literature, history, music, etc.

SEMICOLON REFERENCE GUIDE

When should you use semicolons?

You should use semicolons when you
- combine independent clauses into one compound sentence
- punctuate lists when the listed items include commas

Using Semicolons in Compound Sentences

You can use a semicolon to combine independent clauses and create a compound sentence. You can do this with or without a conjunctive adverb.

Without a conjunctive adverb

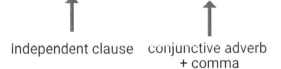

I have a lot of work to do; I don't think I'll be able to go out tonight.

         ↑   ↑

independent clause   independent clause

With a conjunctive adverb

She loves to read; however, she also enjoys playing video games.

independent clause   conjunctive adverb   independent clause
                     + comma

Using Semicolons in a List

We're used to using commas to separate items in a list, but what do we do when the items themselves use commas? That's where the semicolon comes in. Instead of using commas, you replace them with semicolons.

I've lived in Houston, Texas; Chicago, Illinois; and Portland, Oregon.

      ↑   ↑   ↑

Houston, Texas   Chicago, Illinois   Portland, Oregon
is one place.   is one place.   is one place.

You should bring your tent; large, fluffy pillow; and a sleeping bag.

                 ↖ The second item in the list
                     includes a comma.

COLON REFERENCE GUIDE

When should you use colons?

Use colons
- in ratios or when telling time
- to combine independent clauses where the second clause explains the first
- to set off a list or quotation after an independent clause

Using Colons for Time and Ratios

I cook rice with a 2:1 ratio of water to rice.

We need to leave at 12:30 p.m.

Using Colons to Combine Independent Clauses

You can use a colon, instead of a semicolon, to combine independent clauses if the second independent clause explains the first independent clause.

I have two options: I can either stay home and relax or go out with friends.

independent clause   independent clause that
                                   explains the options

Using Colons to Set Off a List or Quote

If a list or quote comes after an independent clause, it should be set off by colon.

Note: If the list or quote is required to complete the independent clause, do not use a colon.

The recipe requires three ingredients: flour, sugar, and eggs.

independent clause   list

She told me something that I'll never forget: "Life is too short to waste time."

independent clause   quote

USING SEMICOLONS

For each sentence, circle any errors with the use of semicolons or missing semicolons.

1. The art exhibit featured works from several artists: paintings by Monet, Van Gogh, and Picasso, sculptures by Rodin and Michelangelo, and photographs by Ansel Adams and Annie Leibovitz.

2. He studied for hours; consequently; he aced the exam.

3. The store was closed today it is also closed tomorrow.

4. The weather was perfect for a picnic therefore, we decided to have lunch outdoors.

5. The bookstore had a wide selection of books: classic literature, such as *Pride and Prejudice* and *To Kill a Mockingbird*, contemporary fiction, such as *Gone Girl* and *The Girl on the Train*; and non-fiction, such as *Becoming* and *Educated*.

In the following sentences, add as many missing semicolons as necessary.

6. Make sure to bring a tent your warm, hooded sleeping bag and a pillow.

7. We had planned to go to the beach instead, we stayed home and watched movies.

8. Choose a sentence from 1-5. Rewrite the sentence correctly on the lines below.

_____

_____

_____

_____

_____

USING COLONS

For each sentence, circle any errors with the use of colons or missing colons.

1. Her grocery list included: bread, coffee, and bananas.

2. The author began his book with a powerful quote, "The only way to do great work is to love what you do."

3. The formula requires a ratio of 1-3.

4. She had a lot of hobbies; painting, knitting, and playing the guitar.

Add a colon to each of the following sentences.

5. The reason for the delay was obvious there was heavy traffic on the highway.

6. You need to mix those at a 3 1 ratio.

7. You need a few supplies pencils, markers, and paper.

8. Choose a sentence from 1-4. Rewrite the sentence correctly on the lines below.

_____

_____

_____

_____

_____

COLONS AND SEMICOLONS

For each sentence, add colons or semicolons where they are needed.

1. He lied to me therefore, I broke up with him.

2. She knew this saying was true today "You win some. You lose some."

3. Know this you're not always right.

4. This meeting had a 3 1 ratio of men to women.

5. This recipe is very simple it only requires bananas, oats, and honey.

6. His travel itinerary includes Paris, France Frankfurt, Germany and Budapest, Hungary.

Combine the following sentences using a semicolon or colon rule.

7. His words echoed long after he left.

I'll never forgive you.

_____

_____

8. I have a doctor's appointment on Tuesday.

Wednesday I need to get my car fixed.

_____

_____

Write a sentence using colon and semicolons rules.

9. Write a sentence using a semicolon and conjunctive adverb.

_____

_____

SEMICOLONS AND COLONS
TEST YOUR KNOWLEDGE

Put an X through any box that has errors with the use of colons and semicolons.

He has a busy schedule: he goes to the gym in the morning; works all day; and takes night classes.	I have a dentist appointment tomorrow; I need to remember to brush my teeth before I go.	This is a good piece of advice: "Believe you can and you're halfway there."	The museum has paintings from the Renaissance; sculptures from ancient Greece; and artifacts from the Middle Ages.
The bus will arrive at 1:45 p.m.	The meeting was long and tedious; however, we were able to come to a decision in the end.	The storm was approaching quickly, we needed to secure the windows and doors.	The concert featured three bands a local indie group, a well-known rock band, and a Grammy-winning artist.
She has many goals for the future, to travel, to learn a new language, and to start her own business.	He is a skilled writer; as a result, his articles have been published in several major newspapers.	The project was challenging nevertheless; we were able to complete it on time and within budget.	The company is expanding its operations: it is opening new offices in Europe and Asia and hiring more employees.
In the study, we found that the ratio of students who preferred online learning to in-person learning was 3:2.	She is an accomplished athlete: she has won several medals in national competitions and holds a world record.	He has a lot of work to do: a report to write, emails to send, and meetings to attend.	Martin Luther King's speeches were inspirational to many, "Darkness cannot drive out darkness; only light can do that. Hate cannot drive out hate; only love can do that."
He loves to travel he has been to over 20 countries in the past year.	The party was a success, everyone had a great time and enjoyed the food and drinks.	The recipe calls for: flour, sugar, and butter.	At the end of the day, Susie was happy with the results; they were just what she needed.

RHETORIC REFERENCE GUIDE

rhetoric: the art of effective or persuasive speaking or writing

rhetorical appeals: emotional, ethical, and logical arguments used for persuasion

  ethos: a rhetorical appeal that focuses on the ethics or qualifications of the speaker

  logos: a rhetorical appeal that uses facts, evidence, and logic to appeal to the audience's sense of reason

  pathos: a rhetorical appeal focused on the audience's emotions

ETHOS   **LOGOS**    **PATHOS**

The Rhetorical Triangle

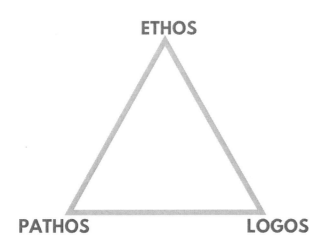

Aristotle provided us with three ways to appeal to an audience: ethos, logos, and pathos.

The relationship between the three appeals and how they are used is often referred to as the rhetorical triangle.

Aristotle believed all three rhetorical appeals need to be present in order to be persuasive. That doesn't mean they need to be used equally. The writer or speaker needs to think about the audience and purpose.

RHETORICAL APPEALS IN ADVERTISING

Use the chart below to examine advertisements for their use of rhetorical appeals. In the first column, write the name of the product being advertised. In the second column, describe the images and messaging of the ad. In the last column, explain how the ad uses each rhetorical appeal.

You can use advertisements from magazines or TV commercials, or you can search for advertisements on the internet.

Product	Describe the ad.	How does the ad use rhetorical appeals?

SELLING WITH RHETORICAL APPEALS

Try to sell this car. Think about who would want this car and how you can use ethos, logos, and pathos to persuade consumers to buy it. Use the box below to create an advertisement for this car. Think about both the images and words that you include.

SELLING WITH RHETORICAL APPEALS

Who did you try to target with your advertisement?

Explain how you used each rhetorical appeal in your advertisement. Use the chart below to list how you used each appeal.

ETHOS	LOGOS	PATHOS

RHETORICAL APPEALS
TEST YOUR KNOWLEDGE

Read each statement and decide if it is using ethos, logos, or pathos. Write the correct rhetorical appeal on the line provided.

_____ 1. Model Cindy Crawford agrees that this is the only wrinkle cream a woman needs.

_____ 2. Wrapping your baby in a Huggies diaper is like wrapping them in a warm hug.

_____ 3. Crest White Strips get your teeth 20% whiter than other leading brands.

_____ 4. Crash tests show that our cars rank number one for safety.

_____ 5. Our company has been trusted for 90 years to bring you quality products.

Match each term to its definition by writing the correct letter on the line provided.

_____ 6. rhetorical appeals

_____ 7. ethos

_____ 8. logos

_____ 9. pathos

_____ 10. rhetoric

a. the art of effective or persuasive speaking or writing

b. emotional, ethical, and logical arguments used for persuasion

c. facts, evidence, and logic to appeal to the audience's sense of reason

d. focuses on ethics or the qualifications of the speaker

e. focused on the audience's emotions

BACKGROUND INFORMATION
STATEMENT ON THE ASSASSINATION OF MARTIN LUTHER KING JR.

A jubilant crowd gathered on the Northside of Indianapolis expecting to hear a campaign speech from Robert Kennedy, who recently declared his candidacy for the democratic presidential nomination. Kennedy, younger brother of slain former president John Kennedy, was preparing to board a plane when he received word that Martin Luther King Jr. had been shot. Upon arriving in Indianapolis, Kennedy was informed that Martin Luther King Jr. had died from t he wounds he received from the assassin's bullet. After making a brief statement to the press at the airport, Robert Kennedy canceled a planned event in downtown Indianapolis but decided to proceed with the speech on the Northside of the city. Numerous city officials, including the mayor, future U.S. Senator Richard Luger, were greatly concerned about this decision. They worried that the presidential candidate's life could be in jeopardy from people wanting revenge for the death of Martin Luther King Jr. All across the United States, riots and protests were breaking out at the news of the assassination.

The speech Kennedy had planned on delivering to the crowd at the Broadway Christian Center was what would be expected from a presidential candidate. In the speech, Kennedy would outline his vision and why he would be better for the country than his opponents. The news of Martin Luther King Jr.'s death forced Kennedy to change his plans. Alone in the backseat of the car, Kennedy struggled with what he would say to the crowd, who were largely unaware of Martin Luther King Jr.'s death. Kennedy jotted down a few notes on the back of an envelope before arriving to the crowd who was anxious to hear from the young presidential candidate.

Wearing a black overcoat that belonged to his older brother John, Robert Kennedy stepped onto the back of a pickup truck where he was to deliver his speech. Just before delivering his remarks, Robert could be heard asking someone if the crowd knew about Martin Luther King Jr.'s death. Kennedy then addressed the crowd, asking them to put their signs down before informing them that Martin Luther King Jr. had been assassinated. As the crowd responded with audible gasps and cries, Kennedy delivered one of his most powerful speeches. Speaking without notes, Kennedy's roughly six minute speech outlined the need for compassion over vengeance and love over hatred. While the speech did not lessen the loss of Martin Luther King Jr., it did lessen any desires for revenge. There were no protests on the Northside of Indianapolis that night where Kennedy delivered his remarks. Sadly, less than two months after delivering these remarks, Kennedy's life would also be cut short from an assassin's bullet.

ROBERT KENNEDY'S SPEECH
STATEMENT ON THE ASSASSINATION OF MARTIN LUTHER KING JR.

I have bad news for you, for all of our fellow citizens, and people who love peace all over the world, and that is that Martin Luther King was shot and killed tonight.

Martin Luther King dedicated his life to love and to justice for his fellow human beings, and he died because of that effort.

In this difficult day, in this difficult time for the United States, it is perhaps well to ask what kind of a nation we are and what direction we want to move in. For those of you who are black--considering the evidence there evidently is that there were white people who were responsible--you can be filled with bitterness, with hatred, and a desire for revenge. We can move in that direction as a country, in great polarization--black people amongst black, white people amongst white, filled with hatred toward one another.

Or we can make an effort, as Martin Luther King did, to understand and to comprehend, and to replace that violence, that stain of bloodshed that has spread across our land, with an effort to understand with compassion and love.
For those of you who are black and are tempted to be filled with hatred and distrust at the injustice of such an act, against all white people, I can only say that I feel in my own heart the same kind of feeling. I had a member of my family killed, but he was killed by a white man. But we have to make an effort in the United States, we have to make an effort to understand, to go beyond these rather difficult times.

My favorite poet was Aeschylus. He wrote: "In our sleep, pain which cannot forget falls drop by drop upon the heart until, in our own despair, against our will, comes wisdom through the awful grace of God."

What we need in the United States is not division; what we need in the United States is not hatred; what we need in the United States is not violence or lawlessness; but love and wisdom, and compassion toward one another, and a feeling of justice toward those who still suffer within our country, whether they be white or they be black.

So I shall ask you tonight to return home, to say a prayer for the family of

ROBERT KENNEDY'S SPEECH
STATEMENT ON THE ASSASSINATION OF MARTIN LUTHER KING JR.

Martin Luther King, that's true, but more importantly to say a prayer for our own country, which all of us love--a prayer for understanding and that compassion of which I spoke.

We can do well in this country. We will have difficult times; we've had difficult times in the past; we will have difficult times in the future. It is not the end of violence; it is not the end of lawlessness; it is not the end of disorder.

But the vast majority of white people and the vast majority of black people in this country want to live together, want to improve the quality of our life, and want justice for all human beings who abide in our land.

Let us dedicate ourselves to what the Greeks wrote so many years ago: to tame the savageness of man and make gentle the life of this world.

Let us dedicate ourselves to that, and say a prayer for our country and for our people.

STATEMENT ON THE ASSASSINATION OF MARTIN LUTHER KING JR.
SOAPSTone CHART

SOAPSTone	
SPEAKER: What do you know about the speaker?	
OCCASION: What is the context and setting?	
AUDIENCE: Who is the target audience for the text?	
PURPOSE: Why did the author write this text?	
SUBJECT: What is the topic of this text?	
TONE: What is the tone of the text?	

RHETORICAL APPEALS CHART

ETHOS How does Kennedy use ethos? Provide examples.	
LOGOS How does Kennedy use logos? Provide examples.	
PATHOS How does Kennedy use pathos? Provide examples.	

STATEMENT ON THE ASSASSINATION OF MARTIN LUTHER KING JR.
LITERARY DEVICES CHART

LITERARY DEVICES	What literary devices does Kennedy use in the speech? Look for things like repetition, metaphor, simile, allusion, anaphora, etc. In the first column, write the name of a literary device. In the second column, write an example from the speech and its purpose.

WRITING A RHETORICAL ANALYSIS

You will be writing a rhetorical analysis for Robert Kennedy's statement on the assassination of Martin Luther King Jr. Think about the purpose for Kennedy's speech and how effective he was in achieving that purpose. Use the questions below to start organizing your ideas for the analysis essay.

What was the purpose of Kennedy's speech?

Do you think he achieved that purpose?

How did he achieve or not achieve that purpose?

Looking back at the speech, what could you use for textual evidence to support your idea?

The following pages have graphic organizers to walk you through your essay paragraph by paragraph.

RHETORICAL ANALYSIS ESSAY
INTRODUCTION

HOOK A hook should catch a reader's attention. It could be a quotation, question, or interesting fact.	
BACKGROUND INFO Share background information explaining the context of the speech and its purpose.	
THESIS Your thesis is the main point you are trying to make. The thesis should clearly state whether or not the speaker achieved his purpose with the use of rhetorical appeals.	

RHETORICAL ANALYSIS ESSAY
BODY PARAGRAPH 1: ETHOS

TOPIC SENTENCE The topic sentence should be the first idea in support of your thesis statement. Be sure to use a transition at the beginning of the paragraph.	
EVIDENCE/SUPPORT Provide evidence of ethos to support what you said in the topic sentence. Use quotations from the speech.	
EXPLANATION OF EVIDENCE/SUPPORT Explain how the evidence you just provided supports the topic sentence and the thesis. Do not just restate a quotation. Explain it.	
CONCLUDING STATEMENT Wrap up your first body paragraph.	

RHETORICAL ANALYSIS ESSAY
BODY PARAGRAPH 2: LOGOS

TOPIC SENTENCE The topic sentence should be the second idea in support of your thesis statement. Be sure to use a transition at the beginning of the paragraph.	
EXPLANATION Explain why the speech lacks logos, and explain how its absence supports the speaker's purpose.	
CONCLUDING STATEMENT Wrap up your second body paragraph.	

RHETORICAL ANALYSIS ESSAY
BODY PARAGRAPH 3: PATHOS

TOPIC SENTENCE The topic sentence should be the third idea in support of your thesis statement. Be sure to use a transition at the beginning of the paragraph.	
EVIDENCE/SUPPORT Provide evidence of pathos to support what you said in the topic sentence. Use quotations from the speech.	
EXPLANATION OF EVIDENCE/SUPPORT Explain how the evidence you just provided supports the topic sentence and the thesis. Do not just restate a quotation. Explain it.	
CONCLUDING STATEMENT Wrap up your third body paragraph.	

RHETORICAL ANALYSIS ESSAY
CONCLUSION

RESTATE THESIS Restate the thesis from the introduction. Do not copy it word for word. Say the same idea in a different way.	
REVIEW MAIN POINTS Review your main points that support your thesis. These should be the ideas in the topic sentences of your body paragraphs.	
CONCLUSION This sentence will conclude the entire essay. This will be your final thought.	

NONFICTION TEXT STRUCTURES REFERENCE GUIDE

 ## WHAT IS TEXT STRUCTURE?

Text structure refers to how the information in a text is organized. The most common text structures are cause and effect, problem and solution, chronological order, descriptive, and compare and contrast. Being able to recognize different text structures can help with comprehension and understanding.

TEXT STRUCTURE	PURPOSE	CLUE WORDS AND PHRASES
CAUSE AND EFFECT	A cause and effect text structure is used to show how one event is the direct cause of other events.	• because • since • as a result • consequently • this led to
PROBLEM AND SOLUTION	A problem and solution text structure is used to address a problem and share possible solutions for the problem.	• problem • answer • solution • question • solve
CHRONOLOGICAL ORDER	A chronological order text structure is used to show a sequence of events or list of steps.	• first • next • then • after
DESCRIPTIVE	A descriptive text structure is used to explain a topic by sharing its features and characteristics and providing examples.	• for example • for instance • in addition • also • such as
COMPARE AND CONTRAST	A compare and contrast text structure is used to show similarities and differences between two or more things.	• different from • same as • similarly • instead of • compared to • however
PROS AND CONS	A pros and cons text structure is used to show the positive and negative aspects of a topic.	• benefits • drawbacks • advantages • disadvantages • trade-offs

NONFICTION TEXT FEATURES REFERENCE GUIDE

WHAT ARE TEXT FEATURES?

Text features are extra visuals or text that help readers to better understand the information. Text features include bold text, footnotes, pictures, captions, charts, diagrams, headings, subheadings, and maps. Text features can provide readers with additional information that is not in the body of the text.

EXAMPLES

MAP

PIE CHART

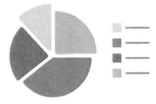

BAR GRAPH

DIAGRAM

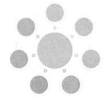

TIMELINE

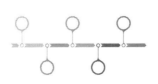

Bold Text

Italics

Highlighted Text

TITLE

Caring for Cats

Cats are beloved pets that require proper care to lead long and healthy lives. Here are some tips for taking care of cats.

Proper Nutrition
Feed your cat a balanced diet that meets their nutritional needs, and ensure your cat has access to clean water at all times.

Grooming
Regularly brush your cat's fur to prevent matting and hairballs.

Litter Box
Clean the litter box daily to avoid unpleasant odors and keep your cat healthy.

Health
Play with your cat regularly to keep them active and healthy. You should also take your cat to the vet at least once a year for routine check-ups and vaccinations.[1]

By following these tips, you can ensure your cat is happy, healthy, and well-cared for.

HEADINGS

PICTURE

CAPTION

A cat visits with his vet for his yearly appointment.

1. Yearly vaccinations are recommended by the Humane Society.

FOOTNOTE

STEALING LINCOLN'S BODY

James 'Big Jim' Kennally, who was known as a "born crook" by a local reporter, was a small-time crime boss who had previously served a five year prison sentence in the Illinois State Penitentiary in Joliet, Illinois for charges related to counterfeiting money. In the 1860s and 1870s, counterfeit currency was a major problem in the United States. It is believed that roughly one-third of the money in circulation in the 1860s was counterfeit.

Ben Boyd was one of the most well-known creators of counterfeit money at the time. After 'Big Jim' Kennally was released from prison, he got back into the business of counterfeit money. He passed the bills made by Boyd to gangs of local criminals for distribution. Kennally served as a middleman for this counterfeiting network.

However, in 1875, Boyd's criminal lifestyle caught up with him, and he was sentenced to ten years in the Illinois State Penitentiary. Knowing the importance of Boyd's role in this counterfeit network, Kennally knew he had to do something drastic. He made the decision that he would get Boyd out of prison. After much deliberation, Kennally came up with a plan. He and a group of associates would steal the body of fallen President Abraham Lincoln and hold it for ransom in exchange for Boyd and two hundred thousand dollars cash.

Lincoln's first burial site at the Oak Ridge Cemetery in Springfield, Illinois.

The associates Kennally chose to carry out this task were named Terrence Mullens and Jack Hughes. Having no experience with stealing a dead body, Mullens and Hughes contacted Lewis Swegles for assistance in this plot, and Swegles happily agreed to help. Unbeknownst to Mullens and Hughes, Swegles was actually an informant for the Secret Service, which was initially formed in 1865 by Abraham Lincoln as an agency to combat counterfeiting. Lewis Swegles swiftly reported the plan to the chief of the Chicago District Office of the Secret Service.

Having been made aware of Kennally's plan, law enforcement agencies, with the help of President Lincoln's one surviving son, Robert, devised a plan to prevent the beloved former president's body from being stolen. It was decided that they would need to catch the criminals in the act of stealing Lincoln's body, so arrangements were made to bring a group of law enforcement officers to Oak Ridge Cemetery in Springfield, Illinois on the night of November 7, 1876.

Working under the cover of darkness, Mullens, Hughes, and the informant Swegles arrived at the cemetery around 9:00 p.m. Swegles discreetly alerted the law enforcement officials of their arrival. Law enforcement had been waiting at the cemetery in multiple locations for two hours. Mullens and Hughes began the tough task of breaking into the burial chamber that held the body of Abraham Lincoln. After picking the lock of the burial chamber,

Abraham Lincoln. After picking the lock of the burial chamber, Mullens, Hughes, and Swegles stood face to face with the sarcophagus that held Lincoln's coffin.

After removing the ornamental marble lid, Mullens and Hughes discovered that the inner lid would not budge. After closer inspection, the inner lid was held in place by a series of copper dowels, which Mullens and Hughes disposed of easily. It was at this point that Swegles told Mullens and Hughes that he was going to get the wagon that was going to be used to transport the body of Lincoln two hundred miles north to the Indiana Dunes, where it would be buried in a secret location.

However, there was no wagon. Swegles left Mullens and Hughes alone to remove Lincoln's lead lined coffin, which was already partially exposed from the sarcophagus, and gave law enforcement officials the signal that it was time to move in and catch them in the act.

Men began racing in from multiple directions to catch the grave robbers. As they were closing in, one of the guns carried by law enforcement accidently misfired. Upon hearing this gunshot, Mullens and Hughes immediately fled the scene, leaving Lincoln's coffin halfway out of the sarcophagus. Neither group of law enforcement officials knew what direction Mullens and Hughes were heading, and when a shadowy group of figures was spotted, a gunfight broke out. After several shots were fired, a realization was made that the gunfight was taking place between the groups of law enforcement. Luckily, no one was injured in the gunfight, but at this point, Mullens and Hughes were long gone.

On November 17, 1876, ten days after the attempted robbery, Mullens and Hughes were caught. They were put on trial and sentenced to one year in solitary confinement in the Illinois State Penitentiary for their crimes.

Concerned for the safety of the coffin holding the body of Abraham Lincoln, the curator of Oak Ridge Cemetery hid the coffin in a crudely dug grave in the burial chamber basement. It was there that the body of the sixteenth president laid until September 26, 1901, when it was given its final burial under ten feet of concrete to ensure there would never again be an attempted theft.

Nonfiction Text Features and Structures

1. Underline the article title.
2. Draw a star next to any captions.
3. Draw a box around the photograph.
4. Draw a triangle next to the map.
5. Underline all years and dates in the article.

STEALING LINCOLN'S BODY

Directions: Read the passage about the attempted theft of Abraham Lincoln's body, and answer each question in complete sentences.

1. Why did James Kennally serve time in prison?

2. What did Kennally do after he got out of prison?

3. Why did Kennally need Boyd out of prison?

4. How did Kennally plan to get Boyd out of prison?

5. What was the biggest mistake that Mullens and Hughes made?

6. Who formed the Secret Service, and what was its original purpose?

7. What did Mullens and Hughes plan to do with Lincoln's body?

8. What mistake did law enforcement make when trying to capture Mullens and Hughes?

9. How did the curator of the cemetery ensure Lincoln's body couldn't be stolen?

10. Why do you think the author included a map of Indiana and Illinois?

11. What text structure is used for this article?

12. Explain how you determined the text structure.

Use information from the article to add dates and events to the blank lines on the timeline.

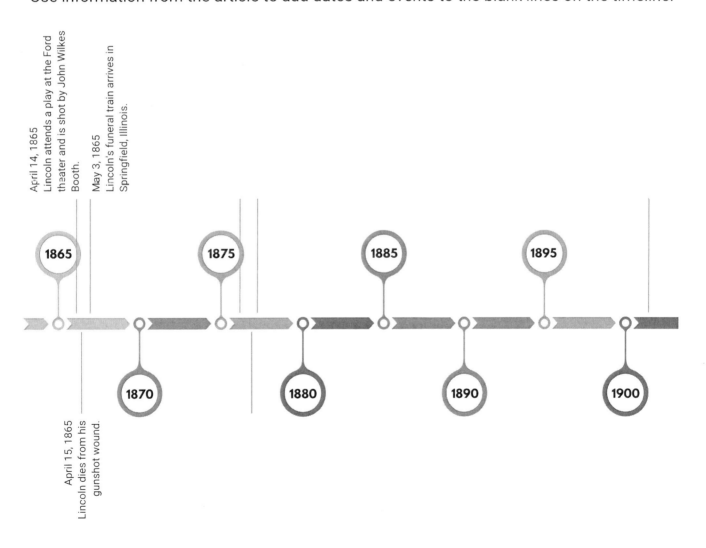

April 14, 1865
Lincoln attends a play at the Ford theater and is shot by John Wilkes Booth.

May 3, 1865
Lincoln's funeral train arrives in Springfield, Illinois.

April 15, 1865
Lincoln dies from his gunshot wound.

1865   1875   1885   1895

1870   1880   1890   1900

Cell Phones in the Classroom: Beneficial or Detrimental?

Cell phones have become ubiquitous[1] in modern society, with individuals relying on them for communication, information access, and various daily tasks. As the prevalence of cell phones continues to grow, so does the debate surrounding their place in classrooms. While there are benefits of the use of cell phones in the classroom, there are also drawbacks.

Access to Information

Cell phones provide students with instant access to many educational resources, including online textbooks, research materials, and educational apps. With the internet at their fingertips, students can quickly and conveniently delve[2] deeper into topics, which promotes independent learning. However, the easy access to information also provides students with the opportunity for cheating and academic dishonesty. Students can easily share answers or engage in other unethical practices during exams. Maintaining academic integrity becomes more challenging when personal devices are present in the classroom.

Productivity

One of the primary concerns regarding cell phones in the classroom is the potential for distractions. Notifications, social media, gaming, and other non-academic apps can divert students' attention away from the lesson and hinder their focus. This can result in decreased learning outcomes

A girl with a cell phone shares with a classmate.

and academic performance. On the other hand, cell phones can serve as valuable tools for organization and productivity. Students can use various apps, such as calendars, note-taking programs, and task managers, to keep track of assignments and deadlines. These digital aids can help students stay organized and manage their workload effectively.

Integration of Technology Skills

Integrating cell phones into the classroom allows students to develop crucial digital literacy and technological skills. By utilizing mobile devices for educational purposes, students become familiar with navigating digital platforms, evaluating online information, and practicing responsible digital citizenship. The issue is that not all students have access to the same quality of cell phones or reliable internet access. This disparity can

---

1. **ubiquitous**: found everywhere
2. **delve**: to try to find more information

create an unequal learning environment, with some students benefiting more from cell phone usage than others. Additionally, students from lower-income backgrounds may face challenges in affording the latest technology, potentially widening the digital divide.

The inclusion of cell phones in the classroom is a complex topic that requires careful consideration of the pros and cons. While cell phones offer access to information, organization tools, and technology skills, they also present challenges related to distractions, academic integrity, and equity.

To find balance, teachers must establish clear guidelines and policies regarding cell phone use in the classroom. This may involve setting designated times for cell phone use, implementing classroom management strategies, promoting responsible digital citizenship, and ensuring equal access to technology resources for all students.

Nonfiction Text Structure

1. Underline the article title.
2. Circle all headings.
3. Draw a star next to any captions.
4. Draw a box around the photograph.
5. Draw an arrow next to any footnotes.

Cell Phones in the Classroom: Beneficial or Detrimental?

Directions: Read the passage about cell phones in classrooms, and answer each question in complete sentences.

1. Use the article footnote to define ubiquitous.

2. While explaining the benefits and hindrances of cell phones in the classroom, what three topics does the article focus on?

3. How is the access to information positive?

4. How is the access to information negative?

5. When cell phones are available in the classroom, what may divert a student's attention from a lesson?

6. Do you feel this article is neutral on the topic of cell phones in class, or do you think it leans more one way than the other? Explain your answer.

7. What text structure does this article follow?

8. What helped you determine the text structure?

Cell Phones in the Classroom:
Beneficial or Detrimental?

Directions: After reading, complete the pros and cons chart below. In the pros column, write the benefits that the article discusses. In the cons column, write the hindrances the article discusses. You are not adding your own thoughts.

PROS	CONS

ARGUMENTATIVE WRITING REFERENCE GUIDE

An **argument** is a debatable issue with two sides.

Argumentative writing focuses on one side of an argument and supports it with evidence.

A **claim** is a writer or speaker's position on an issue.

Evidence is the information that supports or proves an idea or claim such as facts, statistics, examples, etc.

A **counterclaim** is a position taken by someone with an opposing viewpoint.

A **concession** is an admission in an argument that the opposing side has valid points.

A **refutation**, sometimes called a rebuttal, is the reasoning used to disprove an opposing viewpoint.

A **call to action** is what the writer wants the reader to do.

PUTTING IT ALL TOGETHER

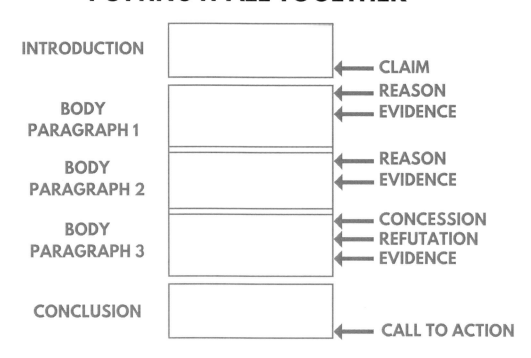

INTRODUCTION — CLAIM

BODY PARAGRAPH 1 — REASON, EVIDENCE

BODY PARAGRAPH 2 — REASON, EVIDENCE

BODY PARAGRAPH 3 — CONCESSION, REFUTATION, EVIDENCE

CONCLUSION — CALL TO ACTION

SAMPLE ARGUMENT ESSAY

Below, you will find a sample argumentative essay about single-sex classrooms. After reading the essay, you will be asked to identify parts of the argument and answer some questions.

Students Successful Apart

Do single-sex classes provide academic benefits? It's a question that many ponder as single-sex classrooms gain popularity in the United States, and they may find there is credibility in this education trend. Single-sex classrooms help children focus on their studies and find academic success.

First, single-sex classes allow students to focus on their work, which increases students' grades. Principal Jill Rojas of Jefferson Leadership Academies in California states, "Student grade point averages for students who had previously attended Jefferson in either grades 6 or 7 increased for all students, male and female, in both grades 7 and 8 under the single gender academy configuration" (Sharpe). Rojas shares that both boys and girls saw an increase in grade point averages when the school switched from co-ed classes to single-sex classes, which should be a goal for all schools. Students with higher grade point averages have more opportunities available to them than those with poor grades.

In addition, single-sex classes can encourage girls to go on to get advanced degrees. Alison Booth, a professor at Australian National University, states, "Women in all-female classes are much more likely to gain a higher degree score and to get a higher-classification degree" (Tasovac). This shows that girls in single-sex classrooms gain more confidence in their intellectual abilities than their counterparts in co-ed classes and take advantage of that to earn advanced degrees.

Some people believe that boys and girls do not have different learning styles, so they belong together in classrooms. However, teachers and administrators who have experienced teaching single-sex classes disagree. Boys and girls have different learning styles and needs. Michael Gurian, author of the book Boys and Girls Learn Differently, states that "gently competitive lessons may be more impactful for boys" and girls need "lessons that incorporate emotions and emotional vocabulary" (Rich). Having single-sex classes allows teachers to provide boys and girls with these lessons that suit their needs. In turn, this means success for all.

To sum up, children succeed in single-sex classrooms because they can focus on their academics. In single-sex classrooms, teachers are better able to provide girls and boys with lessons that suit their learning styles. Students will see increased grade point averages, which leads more girls to earning advanced degrees. For students' academic success, talk with your principal about incorporating single-sex classes in your school.

Works Cited

Rich, Wesley. "Single-Gender Classes. Are They Better?" *Education World*, www.educationworld.com/a_curr/curr215.shtml. Accessed 5 June 2023.

Sharpe, Motoko. "Old Tactic Gets New Use: Public Schools Separate Girls and Boys." *New York Times*, www.nytimes.com/2014/12/01/education/single-sex-education-public-schools-spearate-boys-and-girls.html. Acessessed 5 June 2023.

Tasovac, Brooke. "What's the Benefit of Single-Sex Education?" *Child Mags*, www.childmags.com.au/what-s-the-benefit-of-single-sex-education/. Acessessed 5 June 2023.

EXAMINING AN ARGUMENT ESSAY

Read the argument essay about single-sex classrooms. Then follow the steps in the chart below.

★	Put a star next to the claim.
✓	Put a check mark next to each idea that supports the claim.
underline	Underline evidence used to support the ideas.
△	Put a triangle next to the counterclaim.
⬭	Circle all transition words and phrases.
▭	Put a box around the call to action.

What was done well in this essay? Don't think about your opinion of the topic. Just consider which argument is stronger.

What could improve this essay?

CHOOSING AN ARGUMENTATIVE ESSAY TOPIC

When choosing a topic for your argument essay, be sure that it is a topic that has two sides. Below, list possible topics for your argument.

Final topic choice:

Fill in the pros and cons chart below for your chosen topic. This will help you decide what position you will take on your issue. It will also be helpful when writing your reasoning and counterclaim.

PROS	CONS

The graphic organizers on the next few pages will help you organize your argument essay paragraph by paragraph.

ARGUMENT ESSAY: INTRODUCTION

HOOK

A hook should catch a reader's attention. It could be a quotation, question, or interesting fact.

BACKGROUND INFO

Background information provides readers with any general information about your topic they may need to understand your essay. It could be where you explain why your topic is controversial or why people disagree about it. This is not where you start proving your points.

CLAIM

Your claim is the main argument you are trying to make. It should be the strongest sentence in the essay. All other points you make throughout the paper should support the idea in this one sentence.

ARGUMENT ESSAY: BODY PARAGRAPH 1

TOPIC SENTENCE The topic sentence should be the first idea in support of your claim. Be sure to use a transition at the beginning of the paragraph.	
EVIDENCE/SUPPORT Provide reasons and evidence to support what you said in the topic sentence. You may use quotations from outside sources as evidence, but be sure to cite your sources.	
EXPLANATION OF EVIDENCE/SUPPORT Explain how the evidence you just provided supports the topic sentence and the thesis. Do not just restate a quotation. Explain it.	
CONCLUDING STATEMENT Wrap up your first body paragraph.	

ARGUMENT ESSAY: BODY PARAGRAPH 2

TOPIC SENTENCE The topic sentence should be the second idea in support of your claim. Be sure to use a transition at the beginning of the paragraph.	
EVIDENCE/SUPPORT Provide reasons and evidence to support what you said in the topic sentence. You may use quotations from outside sources as evidence, but be sure to cite your sources.	
EXPLANATION OF EVIDENCE/SUPPORT Explain how the evidence you just provided supports the topic sentence and the thesis. Do not just restate a quotation. Explain it.	
CONCLUDING STATEMENT Wrap up your second body paragraph.	

ARGUMENT ESSAY: BODY PARAGRAPH 3

COUNTERCLAIM This is where you share an opposing argument. This does not support the claim you made in your introduction.	
REFUTATION Argue against the counterclaim. Give a strong reason why the counterclaim is not valid. Do not use the reasons you already used in your first two body paragraphs.	
EVIDENCE/SUPPORT Provide reasons and evidence to support the refutation. You may use quotations from outside sources, but be sure to cite your sources.	
EXPLANATION Explain how the evidence you just provided supports the refutation and the claim. Do not just restate a quotation. Explain it.	
CONCLUDING STATEMENT Wrap up your third body paragraph.	

ARGUMENT ESSAY: CONCLUSION

RESTATE CLAIM Restate the claim from the introduction. Do not copy it word for word. Say the same idea in a different way.	
REVIEW MAIN POINTS Review your main points that support your thesis. These should be the ideas in the topic sentences from body paragraph one and two and the refutation from body paragraph three.	
CONCLUSION This sentence will conclude the entire essay. This will be your final thought.	

POETRY TERMS REFERENCE GUIDE

TERMS	EXAMPLES
POETRY literary work that is written in verse, uses aesthetic and often rhythm	Poetry does not have one definition. It's a literary work that is often rooted in emotion is hard to define.
LINE the units that form stanzas	"So long as men can breathe or eyes can see, So long lives this, and this gives life to thee." **ONE LINE**
STANZA a grouping of lines in a poem, similar to a paragraph in prose	I heard a Fly buzz – when I died – The Stillness in the Room Was like the Stillness in the Air – Between the Heaves of Storm – **} STANZA** The Eyes around – had wrung them dry – And Breaths were gathering firm For that last Onset – when the King Be witnessed – in the Room – **} STANZA**
FIGURATIVE LANGUAGE imaginative language or figures of speech that are not meant to be taken literally	
SIMILE a comparison of two unlike things using the words like or as	She won the race. She ran like a cheetah.
METAPHOR a comparison of two unlike things where one thing is said to be another	She won the race. She was a cheetah.
EXTENDED METAPHOR a metaphor that is drawn out over multiple lines or stanzas	"All the world's a stage, and all the men and women merely players; They have their exits and their entrances; And one man in his time plays many parts."
PERSONIFICATION giving human qualities or actions to a nonliving thing	I was so tired. My bed was screaming my name.

POETRY TERMS REFERENCE GUIDE

TERMS	EXAMPLES
HYPERBOLE extreme exaggeration not to be taken literally	I'm so hungry I could eat a horse.
ONOMATOPOEIA a word that imitates a sound	Buzz. A bee flew by.
ALLITERATION the same sound at the beginnings of words close to one another	Sally sold sea shells by the sea shore.
ANAPHORA the same word or group of words at the beginnings of lines	I feel the grass, I feel the rain, I feel everything.
ASSONANCE repetition of similar vowel sounds in two or more words near each other in a poem	good night, sleep tight
CONSONANCE repetition of similar consonant sounds in two or more words near each other in a line of poetry	Tiffany and Jeffery are staff members.
IMAGERY vivid description or figurative language that helps create mental images	The crisp red and yellow leaves crunched under his soles on the sidewalk. A sudden breeze sent new leaves tumbling from the trees like tiny little parachutes. He watched them swirl in the breeze then skitter across the pavement as the air stilled.
SYMBOL something that has its own meaning but stands for something else on a figurative level	A dove has its own meaning. It's a bird. Figuratively, a dove represents peace.
THEME the main message or lesson of a literary work	Themes are not directly stated in poetry. You have to think about what authors are trying to say with their work.

POETRY TERMS REFERENCE GUIDE

TERMS	EXAMPLES
MOOD the overall atmosphere, the emotion the author tries to evoke from readers	At the most remote end of the crypt there appeared another less spacious. Its walls had been lined with human remains, piled to the vault overhead, in the fashion of the great catacombs of Paris. Three sides of this interior crypt were still ornamented in this manner. **EERIE MOOD**
TONE the author's or speaker's attitude toward a subject	"Do not go gentle into that good night, Old age should burn and rage at close of day; Rage, rage against the dying of the light." **tone:** insistent, desperate He doesn't want his dad to die. He wants him to fight.
REPETITION a word or phrase that repeats within a literary work	To the swinging and the ringing of the bells, bells, bells- Of the bells, bells, bells, bells Bells, bells, bells- To the rhyming and the chiming of the bells!
REFRAIN a line or group of lines that is regularly repeated	"Prophet!" said I, "thing of evil!—prophet still, if bird or devil! By that Heaven that bends above us—by that God we both adore— Tell this soul with sorrow laden if, within the distant Aidenn, It shall clasp a sainted maiden whom the angels name Lenore— Clasp a rare and radiant maiden whom the angels name Lenore." Quoth the Raven "Nevermore." "Be that word our sign of parting, bird or fiend!" I shrieked, upstarting— "Get thee back into the tempest and the Night's Plutonian shore! Leave no black plume as a token of that lie thy soul hath spoken! Leave my loneliness unbroken!—quit the bust above my door! Take thy beak from out my heart, and take thy form from off my door!" Quoth the Raven "Nevermore."
RHYME the repetition of sounds at the ends of words	cat hat
RHYME SCHEME the pattern of end rhyme in a poem	Music to hear, why hear'st thou music sadly? **A** Sweets with sweets war not, joy delights in joy. **B** Why lov'st thou that which thou receiv'st not gladly, **A** Or else receiv'st with pleasure thine annoy? **B**

POETRY TERMS REFERENCE GUIDE

TERMS	EXAMPLES
COUPLET two rhyming lines forming a unit in a poem	"So long as men can breathe or eyes can <u>see</u>, So long lives this, and this gives life to <u>thee</u>."
FORM the structure of a poem such as line length, meter, patterns of rhyme	
FREE VERSE poetry without a set pattern of rhyme or meter	"My voice goes after what my eyes cannot reach, With the twirl of my tongue I encompass worlds and volumes of worlds. Speech is the twin of my vision, it is unequal to measure itself..."
METER regular pattern of stressed and unstressed syllables in a line or stanza	
IAMB a metrical foot consisting of one stressed and one unstressed syllable	above = above
IAMBIC PENTAMETER a line of verse with five metrical feet, each consisting of one unstressed syllable followed by one stressed syllable	"Shall I compare thee to a summer's day?"
CATALOG POEM collection of people, objects, or ideas in list form within poetry	"Come buy, come buy: Apples and quinces, Lemons and oranges, Plump unpeck'd cherries"
HAIKU Japanese form of poetry with three lines, lines one and three have five syllables, line two has seven syllables	Unfocused and tired the bell startled me awake Mondays are hard now

POETRY TERMS REFERENCE GUIDE

TERMS	EXAMPLES
ODE a lyric poem that celebrates or honors a person, place, thing, or idea	ODE TO PUMPKIN PIE The golden crust fit for a king's crown, flaky and buttery, gently cradling the filling, the perfect, fragrant pumpkin.
LIMERICK a humorous poem five lines long with an AABBA rhyme scheme	"There was an old man with a beard, Who said, 'It is just as I feared! Two Owls and a Hen, Four Larks and a Wren, Have all built their nests in my beard!"

SONNET
a 14 line lyric poem with a set pattern of rhyme that is usually written in iambic pentameter
	Shall I compare thee to a summer's day?
	Thou art more lovely and more temperate:
	Rough winds do shake the darling buds of May,
	And summer's lease hath all too short a date;
	Sometime too hot the eye of heaven shines,
	And often is his gold complexion dimm'd;
	And every fair from fair sometime declines,
	By chance or nature's changing course untrimm'd;
	But thy eternal summer shall not fade,
	Nor lose possession of that fair thou ow'st;
	Nor shall death brag thou wander'st in his shade,
	When in eternal lines to time thou grow'st:
	  So long as men can breathe or eyes can see,
	  So long lives this, and this gives life to thee.

RHYTHM the pattern of stressed and unstressed syllables that occurs at a regular pace, thought of as the beat or flow of a poem	

I Never Saw a Moor

by Emily Dickinson

I never saw a moor;
I never saw the sea,
Yet know I how the heather looks
And what a billow be.

I never spoke with God,
Nor visited in heaven.
Yet certain am I of the spot
As if the checks were given.

Vocabulary
moor- open, uncultivated land
heather- a low spreading bush with pink or purple flowers
billow- a large wave or surge of water
check- a slip of paper that a train conductor would give a passenger after taking their ticket

Read the poem and vocabulary. Then answer the questions below.

1. What has the speaker never seen?

2. Despite never having seen these things, what does the speaker know?

3. What comparison is the speaker making in the second stanza?

I Never Saw a Moor

4. How are the first and second stanzas different?

5. What lines are inverted?

FORM
A poem's form is the way it is structured or organized. Think about stanzas, line length, rhyme, rhythm, and other poetic devices. Make a list of things you notice about this poem's form.

TONE
1. The tone of a work is the author or narrator's attitude toward the topic. What is the tone of this poem?

2. Provide at least two lines from the poem that help convey the tone. For each example, explain how the line contributes to the tone.

THEME
1. A theme is the author's message about life. A theme is not just one word. It's a complete idea. What is a possible theme for this poem?

2. What information from the poem helped you determine the theme?

I Never Saw a Moor

ANALYSIS

1. What would be the purpose of discussing never seeing a moor or the sea in the first stanza when the second stanza is about religion?

2. Rewrite lines 3 and 7.

3. Compare lines 3 and 7 to your rewritten lines. Why do you think Dickinson chose to write them that way?

SKETCH

In this poem, the speaker can imagine what places look like without having seen them. Imagine a place that you have never seen, and sketch what it would look like.

place:

I Never Saw a Moor

WRITING PROMPT

Think back to your sketch on the previous page. Write a poem about the place you drew. Like Dickinson's poem, your poem must be two stanzas long with four lines in each stanza. It does not need to follow a specific rhyme scheme. Don't forget to title your poem.

_____

_____

_____

_____

_____

_____

_____

_____

_____

_____

_____

_____

_____

_____

_____

_____

_____

_____

_____

_____

Stopping by Woods on a Snowy Evening

by Robert Frost

Whose woods these are I think I know.
His house is in the village though;
He will not see me stopping here
To watch his woods fill up with snow.

My little horse must think it queer
To stop without a farmhouse near
Between the woods and frozen lake
The darkest evening of the year.

He gives his harness bells a shake
To ask if there is some mistake.
The only other sound's the sweep
Of easy wind and downy flake.

The woods are lovely, dark and deep,
But I have promises to keep,
And miles to go before I sleep,
And miles to go before I sleep.

Read the poem and answer the questions below.

1. What is the speaker doing?

2. What does the horse think?

3. Why does the horse think this?

Stopping by Woods on a Snowy Evening

4. What does the speaker do in the last stanza?

FORM

A poem's form is the way it is structured or organized. Think about stanzas, line length, rhyme, rhythm, and other poetic devices. Make a list of things you notice about this poem's form.

MOOD

Mood is the overall feeling or atmosphere. How does the form of the poem impact its mood? Provide evidence to support your answer.

RHYME SCHEME

A rhyme scheme is a pattern of end rhyme. Rhyme schemes are labeled with letters. The first line is always labeled A. If line two rhymes with line one, it is also labeled A. If it does not rhyme with the first line, it is labeled B. Each new rhyme moves to the next letter of the alphabet. Label the rhyme scheme of the poem on the previous page.

THEME

1. A theme is the author's message about life. A theme is not just one word. It's a complete idea. What is a possible theme for this poem?

Stopping by Woods on a Snowy Evening

2. What information from the poem helped you determine the theme?

SKETCH

Reread the poem and focus on the imagery and descriptive language. Then draw a picture of this scene below.

Stopping by Woods on a Snowy Evening
WRITING PROMPT

Write a poem following the style of "Stopping by Woods on a Snowy Evening." Like Frost's poem, your poem must be four stanzas long with four lines in each stanza. It should follow the AABA BBCB CCDC DDDD rhyme scheme that Frost uses. The topic of your poem is your choice. Don't forget to title the poem.

_____

_____

_____

_____

_____

_____

_____

_____

_____

_____

_____

_____

_____

_____

_____

_____

_____

_____

_____

_____

_____

_____

INDEPENDENT READING NOVEL UNIT

The final unit in the curriculum is an independent reading novel unit. You will read a novel of your choice and complete the book project on following pages. Visit your local public library for a wide selection to choose from.

The novel you choose must be
- fiction
- age appropriate
- over 100 pages long

Please finish your novel before starting on the book project.

NOVEL PLAYLIST BOOK PROJECT

For this book project, you will be creating a playlist for your novel. Each song will have a specific focus. Think about how the lyrics for each song support that focus. You will have to quote lyrics and explain how they fit the novel.

Song 1: Protagonist
The first song on your playlist must reflect the protagonist's personality.

Song 2: Conflict
Your second song must represent the main conflict in the novel. When choosing a song, you can think about the problem itself, how the protagonist responds to the problem, or how it impacts character relationships.

Song 3: Mood
Your third song must reflect the mood at the beginning of the novel. Think about what's happening at the beginning of the novel, how characters are feeling, and where the story is set.

Song 4: Antagonist
The fourth song on your playlist must reflect the antagonist's personality.

Song 5: Setting
The fifth song needs to represent the setting. Think about where most of the novel takes place. Think about the place itself, who is there, what they do there, etc.

Song 6: Theme
The last song will need to represent a major theme from the novel. To find the theme, think about what message the author could be trying to give readers.

Directions:
You will need to carefully choose a song for each focus. On the charts, provide the song title, artist, lyrics relevant to the focus, and an explanation of how that song displays that focus.

For example, the first song needs to reflect the protagonist's personality. You would find a song that represents the protagonist from your novel, quote the lyrics that make you think of that character, and explain how the lyrics show the character's personality.

NOVEL PLAYLIST BOOK PROJECT

Novel Title _____ **Author** _____

SONG 1: Protagonist

SONG TITLE	ARTIST
RELEVANT LYRICS	**EXPLANATION**

SONG 2: Conflict

SONG TITLE	ARTIST
RELEVANT LYRICS	**EXPLANATION**

NOVEL PLAYLIST BOOK PROJECT

SONG 3: Mood

SONG TITLE	ARTIST
RELEVANT LYRICS	EXPLANATION

SONG 4: Antagonist

SONG TITLE	ARTIST
RELEVANT LYRICS	EXPLANATION

NOVEL PLAYLIST BOOK PROJECT

SONG 5: Setting

SONG TITLE	ARTIST
RELEVANT LYRICS	**EXPLANATION**

SONG 6: Theme

SONG TITLE	ARTIST
RELEVANT LYRICS	**EXPLANATION**

ANSWER KEYS

"The Cask of Amontillado" pages 9-18

1. Answers will vary. Samples: full of hate, vengeful, crazy
2. Readers know that Montresor is mad at Fortunato and wants to get revenge.
3. dramatic irony
4. He's happy and celebrating. He's also drunk. He's dressed as a fool or jester.
5. Answers may vary. Sample answer: Running into him is part of his plan to get revenge.
6. Answers may vary. Sample answer: Running into him is part of his plan to get revenge.
7. He wants to try the Amontillado.
8. He's leading him to the family vault below his house.
9. Answers will vary. Sample answer: No, he doesn't mean it. We already know he wants revenge, so he doesn't care about Fortunato being sick.
10. Answers will vary. Sample answer: He's keeping him drunk. Maybe this is so Fortunato doesn't fight back.
11. It's a foot stepping on a snake, and the snake is biting the heel of the foot.
12. Fortunato insulted him somehow, and he swore revenge.
13. The dark, damp vault with bones of dead family members gives the story an eerie feeling. It seems like something bad will happen.
14. Answers will vary. Sample answer: He plans to build something while is down there.
15. He chains him to a wall of the niche.
16. Answers will vary. Sample answers: He's too drunk to resist. He didn't even know Montresor was mad at him, so it was unexpected.
17. Answers will vary. Sample answers: Montresor is crazy. He's cruel. This is part of the torture and revenge.
18. He never tells readers what Fortunato did to make him angry. Maybe Fortunato never did anything wrong.

"The Cask of Amontillado" Irony Chart page 19

Answers will vary. Sample answers:

1. "We will go back; you will be ill, and I cannot be responsible." 2. "My dear Fortunato, you are luckily met. How remarkably well you are looking today!"	1. You aren't leaving, and I'll be responsible for your death. 2. This is perfect. You look drunk enough to take advantage of.
1. Montresor wants to kill Fortunato. 2. Montresor's coat of arms represent his true feelings.	1. Fortunato thinks Montresor wants to share some wine. He thinks they are friends. 2. Fortunato doesn't understand the coat of arms have meaning. It's just small talk.
1. The setting of carnival makes people think of celebrations, not murder. 2. Fortunato thinks he's going to drink expensive wine.	1. Carnival is the perfect time for Montresor to cover up a murder. 2. Montresor kills him while pretending to bring him to the expensive wine.

"The Cask of Amontillado" Writing Prompt page 20

Answers will vary. Sample thesis statements for the topic: 1. In the short story "The Cask of Amontillado," Poe uses verbal irony to build suspense. 2. In Poe's short story "The Cask of Amontillado," he uses dramatic irony to create an eerie mood. 3. In the short story "The Cask of Amontillado," Edgar Allan Poe's use of verbal irony contributes to a surprise ending.

"The Cask of Amontillado" Test Your Knowledge pages 21-22

1. B 2. A 3. B 4. C 5. D 6. B 7. D 8. B

"The Gift of the Magi" pages 23-29

1. It takes place in the early 20th century.
2. Sample answers: "A furnished flat at $8 per week.", "the income was shrunk to $20", "Pennies saved one and two at a time by bulldozing the grocer and the vegetable man and the butcher"
3. She only has $1.87 to buy Jim a Christmas gift, and that isn't enough to get him something nice.
4. They are proud of Jim's watch and Della's long hair.
5. It mentions the Queen of Sheba and King Solomon.
6. Della sells her hair in order to get money for a gift.
7. Answers will vary.
8. She buys him a chain for his watch.
9. Sample answers: Della had to light the gas to use her curling iron. Della mentions Coney Island chorus girls.
10. She's worried that Jim won't think she's pretty anymore without her long hair.
11. He just stares at her. His face is expressionless.
12. Answers will vary.
13. He bought her combs for her hair.
14. This is situational irony.
15. Della bought Jim a chain for his watch, but he sold his watch. Jim bought Della combs for her hair, but she sold her hair. The gifts can't be used.
16. Answers will vary but should relate to sacrificing for another person.

"The Gift of the Magi" Theme Chart page 30

Sample answers: People can show their love by making sacrifices for one another.

"Will you buy my hair?" asked Della. "I buy hair," said Madame. "Take yer hat off and let's have a sight at the looks of it." Down rippled the brown cascade. "Twenty dollars," said Madame, lifting the mass with a practised hand. "Give it to me quick," said Della.	"Dell," said he, "let's put our Christmas presents away and keep 'em a while. They're too nice to use just at present. I sold the watch to get the money to buy your combs. And now suppose you put the chops on."

"The Gift of the Magi" SIFT Chart page 31

Sample answers:

symbol	
"Now, there were two possessions of the James Dillingham Youngs in which they both took a mighty pride. One was Jim's gold watch that had been his father's and his grandfather's."	Because Jim's watch has been passed down, it could symbolize the importance of family and traditions. That shows readers those things are important to Jim.
imagery	
"Pennies saved one and two at a time by bulldozing the grocer and the vegetable man and the butcher until one's cheeks burned with the silent imputation of parsimony that such close dealing implied."	This example shows how important it was for Della to try to save some money.

figurative language "So now Della's beautiful hair fell about her, rippling and shining like a cascade of brown waters."	This simile emphasizes how beautiful Della's hair was.
theme "But in a last word to the wise of these days let it be said that of all who give gifts these two were the wisest. Of all who give and receive gifts, such as they are wisest. Everywhere they are wisest. They are the magi."	This helps develop the theme: people can show their love by sacrificing for one another.

"The Gift of the Magi" Writing Prompt page 32

Sample answer: The theme of O. Henry's short story "The Gift of the Magi" is people can show their love by sacrificing for one another. The irony in the story is shown when Della sells her hair and is given combs as a gift. It's shown again when Jim sold his watch and is given a watch chain as a gift. This irony reinforces the theme because, despite their useless gifts, Jim and Della are still happy. When Della asks for Jim's watch, the text states, "Instead of obeying, Jim tumbled down on the couch and put his hands under the back of his head and smiled." Although Jim knows the watch chain is useless, he's still smiling and happy to be with Della. He appreciates what Della has done for him.

"The Gift of the Magi" Test Your Knowledge pages 33-34

1. B 2. C 3. C 4. D 5. C 6. D 7. D 8. A 9. C 10. B

Using Semicolons page 37

1. The art exhibit featured works from several artists: paintings by Monet, Van Gogh, and Picasso, sculptures by Rodin and Michelangelo, and photographs by Ansel Adams and Annie Leibovitz.

2. He studied for hours; consequently; he aced the exam.

3. The store was closed today it is also closed tomorrow.

4. The weather was perfect for a picnic therefore, we decided to have lunch outdoors.

5. The bookstore had a wide selection of books: classic literature, such as *Pride and Prejudice* and *To Kill a Mockingbird*, contemporary fiction, such as *Gone Girl* and *The Girl on the Train*; and non-fiction, such as *Becoming* and *Educated*.

6. Make sure to bring a tent; your warm, hooded sleeping bag; and a pillow.

7. We had planned to go to the beach; instead, we stayed home and watched movies.

8. Answers will vary.

Using Colons page 38

1. Her grocery list included: bread, coffee, and bananas.

2. The author began his book with a powerful quote, "The only way to do great work is to love what you do."

3. The formula requires a ratio of 1-3.

4. She had a lot of hobbies; painting, knitting, and playing the guitar.

5. The reason for the delay was obvious: there was heavy traffic on the highway.

6. You need to mix those at a 3:1 ratio.

7. You need a few supplies: pencils, markers, and paper.

8. Answers will vary.

Colons and Semicolons page 39

1. He lied to me; therefore, I broke up with him.

2. She knew this saying was true today: "You win some. You lose some."

3. Know this: you're not always right.

4. This meeting had a 3:1 ratio of men to women.

5. This recipe is very simple: it only requires bananas, oats, and honey.

6. His travel itinerary includes Paris, France; Frankfurt, Germany ;and Budapest, Hungary.

7. His words echoed long after he left: "I'll never forgive you."

8. I have a doctor's appointment on Tuesday; Wednesday I need to get my car fixed.

9. Answers will vary.

Semicolons and Colons Test Your Knowledge page 40

He has a busy schedule: he goes to the [gym] in the morning; works all day; and takes night classes. *(crossed out)*	I have a dentist appointment tomorrow; I need to remember to brush my teeth before I go.	This is a good piece of advice: "Believe you can and you're halfway there."	The museum has paintings from the Renaissance; sculptures from ancient Greece; and artifacts from the Middle Ages. *(crossed out)*
The bus will arrive at 1:45 p.m.	The meeting was long and tedious; however, we were able to come to a decision in the end.	The storm was approaching quickly, we needed to secure the windows and doors. *(crossed out)*	The concert featured three bands a local indie group, a well-known rock band, and a Grammy-winning artist. *(crossed out)*
She has many goals for the future, to travel, to learn a new language, and to start her own business. *(crossed out)*	He is a skilled writer; as a result, his articles have been published in several major newspapers.	The project was challenging nevertheless, we were able to complete it on time and within budget. *(crossed out)*	The company is expanding its operations: it is opening new offices in Europe and Asia and hiring more employees.
In the study, we found that the ratio of students who preferred online learning to in-person learning was 3:2.	She is an accomplished athlete: she has won several medals in national competitions and holds a world record.	He has a lot of work to do: a report to write, emails to send, and meetings to attend.	Martin Luther King's speeches were inspirational to many, "darkness cannot drive out darkness; only light can do that. Hate cannot drive out hate; only love can do that." *(crossed out)*
He loves to travel he has been to over [X] countries in the past year. *(crossed out)*	The party was a success, everyone had a great time and enjoyed the food and drinks. *(crossed out)*	The recipe is for: flour, sugar, and butter. *(crossed out)*	At the end of the day, Susie was happy with the results; they were just what she needed.

Rhetorical Appeals in Advertising page 42

Sample answer:

ASPCA	Images of cats and dogs in cages are shown in slow motion. Some of the animals are hurt and bandaged. The screen goes black to show information. A sad, slow song plays in the background. Sarah McLachlan shares about the ASPCA and how to help abused animals.	**Pathos-** The song and images of hurt animals upset viewers. Viewers want to protect these animals. If viewers donate, they are given a welcome package that includes a picture of an animal in a shelter. The picture could help viewers feel a bond to these animals. **Logos-** It shows statistics about how many animals are abused each year. That lets viewers know it's a large scale problem. **Ethos-** They use Sarah McLachlan to share about the ASPCA. If a celebrity is concerned about these animals, viewers should be too.

Selling with Rhetorical Appeals page 43-44

Answers will vary.

Rhetorical Appeals Test Your Knowledge page 45

1. ethos 2. pathos 3. logos 4. logos 5. ethos 6. B 7. D 8. C 9. E 10. A

Statement on the Assassination of Martin Luther King Jr. pages 47-48

Sample annotations:

SOAPSTone Chart page 49

Sample answers:

S	The speaker is Robert F. Kennedy, a U.S. senator who was running for president. He is also the brother of former U.S. President John F. Kennedy, who was assassinated.
O	Kennedy was going to give a speech for his presidential campaign, but his focused changed when he heard the news of MLK's assassination. He gave the speech on the back of a pickup truck on the Northside of Indianapolis, Indiana.
A	The audience was mostly African Americans living in the Indianapolis area.
P	The purpose was to share the news of the assassination of Martin Luther King Jr. Speaking to the audience about this tragic situation could prevent riots in Indianapolis, Indiana.
S	The subject is the death of Martin Luther King Jr. and how they should move forward as a group to reach the goals that King had wanted.
TONE	The tone is somber.

Rhetorical Appeals Chart page 50

Sample answers:

ETHOS	"Or we can make an effort, as Martin Luther King did, to understand and to comprehend, and to replace that violence, that stain of bloodshed that has spread across our land, with an effort to understand with compassion and love." He used MLK's mission to encourage the crowd to respond to the news in a nonviolent way. "My favorite poet was Aeschylus. He wrote: 'In our sleep, pain which cannot forget falls drop by drop upon the heart until, in our own despair, against our will, comes wisdom through the awful grace of God.'" Perhaps he's using the famous poet's words to provide a sense of hope.
LOGOS	He doesn't use logos much in this speech. It was an emotional topic, and ethos and pathos were better suited to connect with the audience.
PATHOS	"For those of you who are black and are tempted to be filled with hatred and distrust at the injustice of such an act, against all white people, I can only say that I feel in my own heart the same kind of feeling. I had a member of my family killed, but he was killed by a white man." He's telling the audience that he can relate to what they are feeling. "But the vast majority of white people and the vast majority of black people in this country want to live together, want to improve the quality of our life, and want justice for all human beings who abide in our land." He's giving the audience some hope and encouragement for the future.

Literary Devices Chart page 51

Sample answers:

parallelism	"What we need in the United States is not division; what we need in the United States is not hatred; what we need in the United States is not violence or lawlessness; but love and wisdom, and compassion toward one another, and a feeling of justice toward those who still suffer within our country, whether they be white or they be black." Beginning each section with "what we need" puts emphasis on the changes that need to occur. It puts emphasis on what is best for everyone moving forward.
repetition	"We can do well in this country. We will have difficult times; we've had difficult times in the past; we will have difficult times in the future." The repetition of the word "we" unifies everyone. It let the crowd know that everyone was in this together.
repetition	"Let us dedicate ourselves to what the Greeks wrote so many years ago: to tame the savageness of man and make gentle the life of this world. Let us dedicate ourselves to that, and say a prayer for our country and for our people." Ending with the repetition of "let us dedicate ourselves" could be a strategy to control how people behave once they leave. It could help promote non violent reactions to this tragedy.

"Stealing Lincoln's Body" Nonfiction Text pages 61-62

1. Underline "Stealing Lincoln's Body."
2. Put a star next to "Lincoln's first burial site at the Oak Ridge Cemetery in Springfield, Illinois.
3. Put a box around the photograph on page 61.
4. Put a triangle next to the map on page 62.
5. Underline 1860s and 1870s, 1860s, 1875, 1865, November 7, 1876, November 17, 1876, and September 26 1901.

"Stealing Lincoln's Body" Questions and Timeline pages 63-64

1. He served prison time because he was charged with crimes related to counterfeiting.
2. He become a middleman for a counterfeiting operation. He took Boyd's counterfeit bills and distributed them to gangs of local criminals.
3. Boyd was the man making the counterfeit bills. Without Boyd, there was no counterfeiting ring. Kennally would be out of a job without Boyd.
4. He planned to have Lincoln's body stolen and would hold it ransom for Boyd's freedom and $200,000.
5. They brought in Lewis Swegles to help, but he was an informant for the Secret Service.
6. Lincoln formed the Secret Service during his presidency to combat counterfeiting.
7. They planned to take the body across state lines and bury it at the Indiana Dunes.
8. Someone's gun misfired alerting Mullens and Hughes, and the police accidentally ended up in a shootout against themselves.
9. He hid the body below the burial chamber basement until 1901. When moved to his final resting place, Lincoln's grave was buried under ten feet of concrete.
10. Answers will vary. Sample answers: It shows readers how far Mullens and Hughes would have to transport Lincoln's body. It marks all of the key places mentioned in the article.
11. The text structure is chronological order.
12. Answers will vary.

Timeline additions: 1.1875: Boyd is arrested and sentenced to ten years in prison. 2. November 7, 1876: The group of criminals try to steal Lincoln's body. 3. November 17, 1876 Mullens and Hughes are caught and arrested. 4. September 26, 190: Lincoln's body is moved to its final resting place.

"Cell Phones in the Classroom: Beneficial or Detrimental?" Nonfiction Text pages 65-66

1. Underline "Cell Phones in the Classroom: Beneficial or Detrimental?" 2. Circle Access to Information, Productivity, and Integration of Technology Skills. 3. Draw a star next to "A girl with a cell phone shares with a classmate. 4. Draw a box around the picture of the girls.

5. Put arrows next to ubiquitous and delve at the bottom of the page.

"Cell Phones in the Classroom: Beneficial or Detrimental?" Questions page 67

1. If something is described as ubiquitous, it means it can be found everywhere.
2. It addresses access to information, productivity, and integration of technology skills.
3. Students can easily access online textbooks, research materials, and educational apps.
4. Students can easily cheat, share answers, or engage in other unethical practices.
5. They can be distracted by notifications, social media, games, and other non-academic apps.
6. Answers will vary.
7. It's a pros and cons text structure.
8. The article discusses both the negative and positive aspects of cell phone use in classrooms.

"Cell Phones in the Classroom: Beneficial or Detrimental?" Pros and Cons page 68

PROS	CONS
• provide students with instant access to many educational resources, including online textbooks, research materials, and educational apps • cell phones can serve as valuable tools for organization and productivity • students can use various apps, such as calendars, note-taking programs, and task managers to keep track of assignments and deadlines • cell phones in the classroom allow students to develop crucial digital literacy and technological skills • students become familiar with navigating digital platforms, evaluating online information, and practicing responsible digital citizenship	• easy access to information provides students with the opportunity for cheating and academic dishonesty • students can easily share answers or engage in other unethical practices during exams • notifications, social media, gaming, and other non-academic apps can divert students' attention away from the lesson • not all students have access to the same quality of cell phones or reliable internet access • students from lower-income backgrounds may face challenges in affording the latest technology, potentially widening the digital divide

Examining an Argument Essay pages 70-72

Students Successful Apart

Do single-sex classes provide academic benefits? It's a question that many ponder as single-sex classrooms gain popularity in the United States, and they may find there is credibility in this education trend. Single-sex classrooms help children focus on their studies and find academic success.

First, single-sex classes allow students to focus on their work, which increases students' grades. Principal Jill Rojas of Jefferson Leadership Academies in California states, "Student grade point averages for students who had previously attended Jefferson in either grades 6 or 7 increased for all students, male and female, in both grades 7 and 8 under the single gender academy configuration" (Sharpe). Rojas shares that both boys and girls saw an increase in grade point averages when the school switched from co-ed classes to single-sex classes, which should be a goal for all schools. Students with higher grade point averages have more opportunities available to them than those with poor grades.

In addition, single-sex classes can encourage girls to go on to get advanced degrees. Alison Booth, a professor at Australian National University, states, "Women in all-female classes are much more likely to gain a higher degree score and to get a higher-classification degree" (Tasovac). This shows that girls in single-sex classrooms gain more confidence in their intellectual abilities than their counterparts in co-ed classes and take advantage of that to earn advanced degrees.

Some people believe that boys and girls do not have different learning styles, so they belong together in classrooms. However, teachers and administrators who have experienced

teaching single-sex classes disagree. Boys and girls have different learning styles and needs. Michael Gurian, author of the book *Boys and Girls Learn Differently*, states that "gently competitive lessons may be more impactful for boys" and girls need "lessons that incorporate emotions and emotional vocabulary" (Rich). Having single-sex classes allows teachers to provide boys and girls with these lessons that suit their needs. In turn, this means success for all.

To sum up, children succeed in single-sex classrooms because they can focus on their academics. In single-sex classrooms, teachers are better able to provide girls and boys with lessons that suit their learning styles. Students will see increased grade point averages, which leads more girls to earning advanced degrees. For students' academic success, talk with your principal about incorporating single-sex classes in your school.

Answers from page 72 will vary.

Choosing an Argumentative Essay Topic page 73
Answers will vary.

"I Never Saw a Moor" Questions pages 84-86
Answers will vary. Sample answers: 1. The speaker has never seen a moor or the sea. 2. Even though the speaker hasn't seen them, she knows what they look like. 3. The speaker compares dying and going to Heaven to riding a train. 4. The first stanza is about the living world. The second stanza is about the afterlife. 5. lines 3 and 7

Form Examples: two stanzas, four lines in each stanza, use of end rhyme (sea, be), one inverted line in each stanza (lines 3 and 7), use of anaphora (I never), rhyme scheme ABCB DEFE, alliteration (billow be)

Tone 1. The tone is confident. 2. Line three says, "Yet know I how the heather looks." Line seven says, "Yet certain am I of the spot." Using words like "know" and "certain" shows confidence. She doesn't have doubts in what she knows. She believes it to be true.

Theme 1. A person doesn't need to experience something first hand in order to understand it. 2. When the speaker describes a moor and the sea, she uses the words "I know." Despite having never seen a moor or the sea, she knows what they would look like. There's confidence in saying "I know."

Analysis 1. She uses never having seen a moor or the sea but knowing what they look like as a way to explain how she can believe in Heaven without having seen it. 2.Yet I know how the heather looks Yet I am certain of the spot 3. Some students may say it impacts the rhythm. Others may say she is putting emphasis on the words know and certain. The emphasis would be taken away if it was rewritten.

"Stopping By Woods on a Snowy Evening" Poem and Questions pages 88-90

1. He stopped to watch the snow fall on the woods. 2. The horse thinks he stopped by mistake. 3.There's no farmhouse or anything nearby, and it's late. The horse doesn't know why he stopped. 4. Although the woods look pretty, he moves on because he has obligations. Form Examples: four lines, four lines in each stanza, pattern of rhyme, rhythm with stressed and unstressed syllables, lines about the same length, repetition in the last two lines, some alliteration, 16 lines total

Mood: Some students may say the mood is calm because of the diction and provide description as evidence. Some students may say it's light-hearted because the rhythm and rhyme make it sound pretty when read aloud.

Rhyme Scheme: AABA BBCB CCDC DDDD

Theme Samples: 1. Our obligations keep us from enjoying simple pleasures. 2. People need to take a break from busy schedules to enjoy the simple things.

Connect with the author:
writeandreadteacher.com
@writeandreadteacher

Made in United States
Cleveland, OH
29 November 2024

11038495R10059